GOLF DOCTOR

GOLF DOCTOR

by
CARY MIDDLECOFF

NICHOLAS KAYE
LONDON

First published in Great Britain by
Nicholas Kaye and Company, Trebeck Street, London, W.1
1952

Printed for Nicholas Kaye and Company at the St Ann's Press, Park Road, Altrincham, and entirely produced in Great Britain

ACKNOWLEDGMENTS

To President L. B. Icely of Wilson Sporting Goods Company—for his foresight in signing up such a crude performer to his fine staff of professionals and for his patience during my necessary period of development.

To professionals J. C. Fondren and O'Neil (Buck) White—for their years of tireless labour on my behalf, developing my game from that of the rawest beginner.

To champion Lloyd Mangrum—for unselfishly passing on to me his knowledge of golf gained through many years of experience on the tournament circuit.

To my father, Dr. H. F. Middlecoff—for his invaluable encouragement in making my decision to shift from dentistry to golf as a profession.

To Memphis Country Club, Chickasaw Country Club, and Colonial Country Club—for putting up with me at a brash age and for replacing, without complaint, all the turf I dug up as a youngster.

To Bob Hope—a great guy and a better golfer than Bing will admit—for helping me with this book.

To photographer Ed Feeney of the *Chicago Tribune* —for sacrificing his week-ends towards making the pictures for this book.

To Mark Cox of Wilson Sporting Goods Company —for his counsel and assistance in planning and writing this book.

CONTENTS

PREFACE

When I became fortunate enough to win the United States National Open golf championship over Medinah Country Club's strenuous No. 3 course near Chicago in June, 1949, several publishers approached me with regard to writing a book. My reaction was that I wasn't qualified to write a book on golf—I just hadn't played the game long enough to pose as an authority.

However, reasoned my friends and would-be publishers, I did play the game well enough to win the National Championship. So, even though I refused to consider myself as a golf authority, why not put down in writing how I played the game—and let the readers decide for themselves whether my methods were good enough to save them strokes if applied to their own games?

In the following pages I will attempt to tell you exactly how I *think* I play the game. I don't want to leave the impression with you that my methods constitute the only sound approach to golf. It is only that the golfing form I am going to describe has proved successful for me. I sincerely hope it will help your game, as well.

Right now, golf to me is a much less complicated game than most professionals and amateurs try to make it. I think a sound golf swing is essential to good, consistent play, and a sound golf swing can be developed almost completely by the proper grip and stance.

A study of golf in the building or developing of a swing reminds me very much of my first year in dental school. I went right into the study of gross anatomy, histology and physiological chemistry in the first quarter. Needless to say, I knew nothing about any of it. Then, all of a sudden, the gross anatomy of the body, its cellular and chemical make-up, began to tie up. I began to see what made it work and why.

As you read this book, I hope you will begin to see how one piece of the golf swing fits in with the rest. Though a golf swing is certainly not to be compared with the human body as a complicated mechanism, some of its parts are just as important to its working correctly as are the bones and nerves of the human body.

In this book you will see, I think, that a golf swing is built almost completely around the proper grip and stance. To me, the grip and stance play the same part in the golf swing that the heart does in the human body. The body has no chance to work unless the heart works. You have little chance of possessing a successful golf swing if your grip and stance are wrong.

In this book I will attempt to show why I think a great deal of the complicated or impossible manoeuvres the average golfer is told to perform can be taken care of easily. The final result can be accomplished simply by standing correctly to the ball and holding the club the right way.

I'm going to start with putting and work back from the hole to the tee. That is my idea of the best way to learn the game. The easiest shot in golf is a 1-inch putt—the toughest is a long, straight drive. So, let's follow the simple, elementary method—just as you started your schooling in kindergarten and advanced through school to college, instead of the other way around.

Even before starting to improve your game, I think it is most important that you have first-class equipment. This is not an attempt to sell you a new set of clubs, for I am sure many of you already are playing with top-notch equipment. However, I know none of you uses inferior materials in your business operations. So why should you do so in golf?

Have your own professional approve your selection of clubs before purchasing them. You should have confidence in him—and if you do, trust his judgment. He can tell you which clubs best fit your requirements from points of length and whip of the shaft, swing, weight, etc.

Now let's get on with the game.

CHAPTER I

PUTTING

PUTTING IS a game in itself. From 30 to 50 per cent of your strokes (depending on your score) are used on the greens, so a close study of the proper putting technique is necessary to a successful game of golf. Often the difference between victory and defeat—whether the match involves professionals or week-end golfers—is decided with the putter.

Putting is the one phase of golf in which practically no concrete ideas have been proved necessarily successful, even in a majority of cases. Every golfer must realize it is entirely possible to play 18 holes of golf, hit every putt of more than a foot in practically perfect form, and still not drop one of them. You must appreciate, however, that over a full season of golf the man who hits the largest percentage of putts the same way, and correctly, will make more putts successfully than the man who is constantly guessing and never hitting the same way twice.

First and foremost in successful putting, a player must make up his mind before addressing the putt exactly on what line he is going to attempt to hit it. Many more putts are missed from an indefinite mental picture of where the ball is supposed to go than from faulty strokes. When a person doesn't know whether the putt is going to stop 2 inches or 6 inches from the hole, he just "wishes" at it instead of hitting it good and firm.

Every golfer should approach each putt with at least a definite picture of the *direction* he will attempt to hit the ball and the *distance* he wants his putt to roll. I think distance and direction are equally important. Distance is more important when you are playing a different course every day, as we do on the tournament circuit. But when you play the same course most of the time, they are equally important because you know the distance automatically.

A putt should be surveyed in two different sections, I believe. First, take a side view of your putt and get firmly entrenched in your mind whether you think it will be a slow putt, a fast putt, or just a medium putt. Secondly, from behind the ball pick out your intended line. Then, without changing your mind, make your putt.

An excellent way to judge the speed of your putt is to study the grass in a 3- or 4-foot circle around the hole. If the grass looks heavy and stubby, you know you can safely take a pretty good rap at the putt. However, if the grass around the hole looks bare and worn, then you are better off to go gently at the hole. More than any other one thing I know, this will prevent three-putting.

SELECTION OF A PUTTER

It certainly does not seem logical to assume that a person 5 feet 4 inches tall would use the same length putter as a person 6 feet tall.

In my own experience, I have found that by using a putter about $2\frac{1}{2}$ inches longer than regulation, I have putted much better than I ever did with the regulation length putter.

In the summer of 1948, I was putting so badly in the tournaments that I was almost desperate enough to quit professional golf. Talking to my close friend Lloyd Mangrum one night in a Detroit hotel, I poured out all my troubles like a bucket of water. Lloyd told me if I would get a longer shafted putter and give it a two- or three-week trial, he would almost guarantee I would putt better.

The main reason for this variation in putter length is to facilitate getting your head and eyes directly over the ball when preparing to hit your putt. I cannot think of one good putter on the professional tour who does not have his eyes directly over the ball. *This is the one point on which I can definitely say all good putters agree.*

Another factor in the longer shafted putter which seemed to help me was that I could, by simply turning my eyes, see the entire track from my ball to the hole. In a crouched position, bent over the ball, I had to turn my whole head and shoulders to survey the line of a long putt when I used the shorter putter.

Such a total movement frequently is enough to throw you off balance and give you a false line to the hole.

PUTTING GRIP

Any golfer who ever stepped into a locker room has heard the merits of many individual putting grips

This is how an unusually tall person looks with a putter too short for him. Note that his eyes are not directly above the ball but about 6 inches over and beyond it. The player is forced to crouch and cannot gain a true conception of the putt.

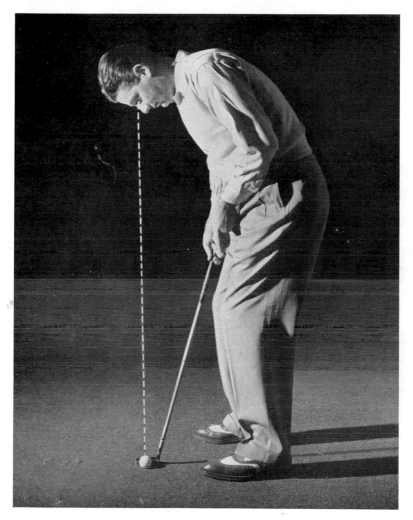

Here is the same size player using a putter of correct length.
The posture is straighter and more comfortable, and the eyes
are directly over the ball.

extolled. Actually, I cannot truthfully say any one putting grip is infallible, or even nearly so. However, the most widely used putting grip has been most successful for me.

This is a grip with the club running diagonally from the second joint of the left forefinger and over the thickest part of the hand. The shaft almost rests in the crevice of the heel of the hand just below the wrist.

The right hand takes almost entirely a finger grip, with the two hands being joined together by the forefinger of the left hand resting across, or over, the last

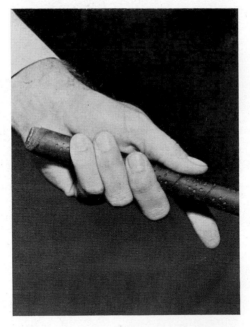

Side view of putter grip for the left hand. The end of the grip rests on the heel of the hand, almost in the groove of the palm below the wrist.

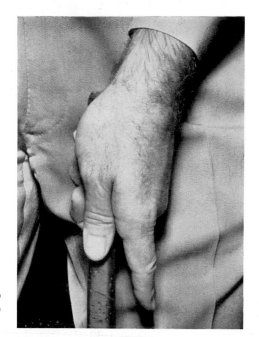

n this front view of the putting grip
of the left hand note that the thumb
points straight down the shaft.

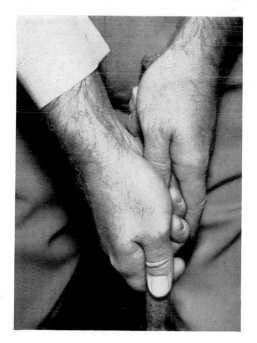

This front view of both hands gripping
the putter shows the thumbs of both
hands pointing down the shaft. The
fore finger of the left hand also is overlapping the last three fingers of the right
hand.

19

three fingers of the right hand. This is called a reverse overlap.

I prefer to have both thumbs running directly down the top of the shaft. With the thumbs running directly down the top, the back of the left hand and the palm of the right hand face almost directly at the hole.

By the use of this type of grip, the wrists seem to co-ordinate better. However, I must admit that I have seen many good putters successfully employ variations of this grip.

PUTTING STANCE

I prefer to stand with both feet forming a right angle with the line to the hole, and with both feet about square to that desired putting line. In other words, the toes of both feet are at equal distance from the intended line.

I definitely think that a slight variation of stance should be employed for right-breaking and left-breaking putts.

In stroking a putt breaking from right to left, I think the ball should be played more toward the centre of the two feet than toward the left toe, as on normal putts. This is due to the natural opening and closing action of the putter on the backswing and follow-through. With the ball played farther back, the golfer has a better chance of hitting it before the face of the putter begins to close. This definitely gives him a better chance to keep the ball up the hill on the intended line.

For a putt breaking from left to right, I would recommend the exact opposite. That is, by playing the ball closer to the left toe than normal and hitting the

This is my stance for a straight putt. Notice that the ball is played just inside the left heel for a putt that is straight or almost straight.

ball either with the putter square to the line, or before the face has begun to close, the player once again has the best chance to keep the ball above the cup on the intended line.

For straight putts, I prefer first a comfortable stance. For me that stance has been with the ball played just inside the left heel. Then the variation we spoke of on side-hill putts would be about 1 or 1½ inches to either side for a straight putt.

I have analysed the results of this system very closely in tournament play and found that although I could not account for any definite difference in the number of putts made on any one round, I did save an average of two or three strokes over the four rounds of a 72-hole tournament.

TYPES OF STROKES

Going back to my original theory of consistency in putting, I think an individual should establish one definite way to putt and use that method all the time.

However, I must confess that I have changed several times myself and still find no particular advantage in either of the two types I am about to mention.

I. COMPLETELY WITH THE WRISTS:

With this type of putting, I found I holed more long putts. There seems to be a little better touch. On the other hand, I found I also yanked more short putts.

When putting entirely with the wrists, concentrate on completely immobilizing every other part of your body. An excellent aid in guiding the putter head during this type of stroke is freezing the right elbow against the right side during the entire putt. This places a definite guide on the wrists and practically eliminates missing putts to the left side of the hole. I recommend this type of putt for extremely fast greens.

2. WITH ABSOLUTELY STIFF WRISTS:

I have found this type of putting stroke excellent for putts of 6 feet and under, but as the putts get longer, there seems to be less touch in your stroke. That is, the correct distance is harder to attain.

It is almost impossible to putt either way without at least a slight variation of the other. Still, I definitely do not recommend a combination of the two types of putting. Choose—and stick to—one or the other.

The one item which should always be in the mind of the person putting is that good stroking consists of only one element—and that is *bringing the putter back to its starting position during the stroke* That is a matter everybody forgets—even the most seasoned pros.

If you should feel I have spent too much space on putting, please remember that 30 to 50 per cent of the strokes in a round of golf are executed on the greens. Putting and driving as a combination form 50 to 70 per cent of the game of golf.

This photo shows the backswing for a straight putt. Notice that nothing has moved in bringing the putter back except the hands and the forearms. No other movement is necessary.

A split second after contact with the ball, nothing except the hands and forearms has moved. The club head has merely been returned to the starting point and has met the ball. The body remains stationary, except for the movement of the hands and forearms.

Completion of the putting stroke, or the follow-through, is simply a continuation of the movement which brought the putter back to its starting position. In this part of the stroke we see again that only the hands and forearms move.

A study in expression—National Open Champion Cary Middlecoff striding to the 72nd tee at Medinah Country Club for his final hole in the 1949 Open.

CHAPTER II

GRIP AND STANCE, AS THEY RELATE TO THE ENTIRE SWING

ALLOW ME to revert to fundamentals again and attempt to impress you with the fact that *the proper grip and stance for each individual are the keys to a sound golf swing.*

GRIP

There are several accepted ways to hold a golf club, but I have very little respect for any great variation from the Vardon overlapping grip. This is simply because every good player, with almost no exceptions, has used the Vardon overlap or a very slight variation during his tournament-winning days.

The Vardon overlapping grip has the club running diagonally across the left hand from the second joint of the left forefinger and coming out across the middle of the thick part of the heel of the hand. It is a combination palm and finger grip.

The left thumb runs down the shaft and about one-fourth the distance over the top of the shaft on the side of the right shoulder. Thus, the left thumb and portion of the hand above the knuckle of the left forefinger form a V. This V should point about to the right shoulder, and if properly formed, will show two or three knuckles of the left hand when the player looks down the shaft of the club to the ball.

27

The grip of the right hand is a complete finger grip, with the little finger of the right hand overlapping the forefinger of the left. The thumb of the right hand runs down the shaft about one-fourth the distance over the top of the shaft on the side of the left shoulder. The thumb and forefinger of the right hand form a V almost exactly the same as the V of the left hand and parallel to it. This V also should point to the right shoulder.

The thumb of the right hand should be in close union with the end of the right forefinger.

All fingers on both hands should be in close union with one another, though not cramped. The club should be held firmly in both hands, though not to the point that either upper arm is tense. You might visualize the grip as similar to one you take on your knife and fork. It is a firm, definite grip, but not one you would take on the rear of a car to lift it.

One of the variations of this grip that is sometimes helpful is an interlocking of the left forefinger and right little finger. This is very good for people with small hands. The purpose of interlocking or overlapping is to join the hands closer together so they can work more closely in unison.

A few players have very successfully used the interlocking grip with the left thumb off the shaft of the club. Usually this grip is adopted by a player who has been forced to use it because of an injury to his thumb, or some type of deformity. The leverage and guiding ability furnished by the left thumb on the shaft of the club are almost indispensable.

There is only one grip necessary for every stroke,

from a chip shot all the way through the drive. No variations are needed.

Watch your grip very closely and check it before every shot. You will find that with the left hand too far over the top of the shaft and the right hand too far under the shaft, a hooked ball is almost sure to result. Conversely, with the left hand too far under the shaft and the right hand too far over, a slice is the customary result.

I believe any individual, by just letting his hands hang normally at his sides, will see they hang straight down—which is the natural way. Therefore it would not be logical to turn either or both hands off at an angle and expect to accomplish results as good as you would get by the natural position.

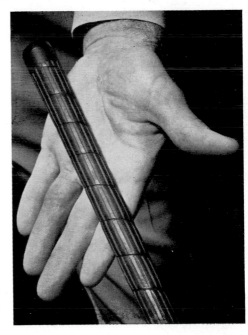

The first step in gripping the club for all other shots except putting is to place the club diagonally across the fingers and palm of the left hand.

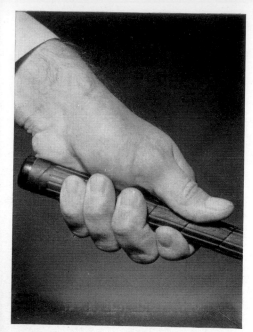

The side view of the left hand gripping the club shows the thumb contacting the club almost on the joint of the thumb.

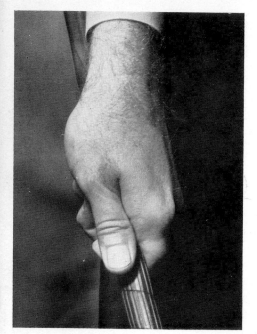

The thumb and the rest of the left hand are joined closely together in this front view of the left hand grip. Also note that the thumb is resting slightly on the side of the shaft and not directly on the top.

Back view of the two hands joined together, gripping the club. The little finger of the right hand is overlapping the forefinger of the left hand.

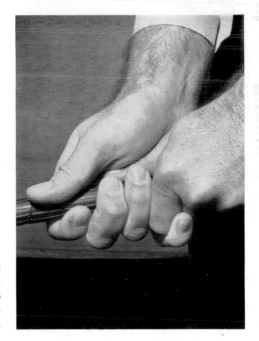

In this side view of the two hands on the club, note that the grip of the right hand is completely in the fingers. The thumb of the left hand is resting snugly in the groove of the heel of the right palm.

31

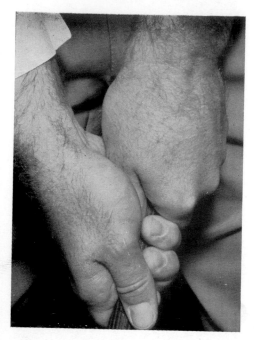

The Vs formed by the thumb and fir finger of each hand are parallel an both point in the same direction—ove the right shoulder. The first tw knuckles of the left hand are plainl visible. The thumb of the right han rests slightly on the left side of the clu and not directly on top.

STANCE

The stance varies slightly with almost every club. To make sure the reader understands the terminology, " square stance," " open stance," and " closed stance," I will describe each of them briefly.

Square Stance This is a stance taken with the toes of both feet equally distant from the direction line of the ball to the flag.

Open Stance This is a stance taken with the left foot farther from the direction line to the flag than is the right foot, and with the entire body partly facing in the general direction of the flag.

Closed Stance This is a stance with the right foot farther from the direction line than is the left foot and with the entire body facing slightly away from the flag.

On the following pages are illustrations of the correct

This is the square stance, with both feet
touching the direction line.

This is the open stance. The left foot
is withdrawn from the direction line.

C   33

stance taken with each club, starting with the No. 9
You will notice in these pictures that the stance shifts
almost exactly to the opposite as we go from the 9
iron up to the driver.

This is the closed stance, with the right
foot withdrawn from the direction line.

You also will notice that an open stance, with the
feet relatively close together, is employed in the short
irons. This gradually progresses to a wider and squarer
stance and then to a maximum-width stance that is
slightly closed with the driver.

With the shortest irons, there is a premium on accuracy, and most of the body movement should be
eliminated. As the stance gradually gets wider and
squarer, the shots are longer and, though we are still

34

Side view of a player contacting the ball from an improper closed stance. The club is swinging well to the right of the intended line of direction. Also note the position into which the shoulders and lower part of the body are forced. The alignment of the feet makes it difficult to do otherwise.

Here is the same side view of the player using an incorrect open stance. The line of the shoulders and hips is badly out of line to the left of the intended direction, as a result of the poor position of the feet. This shot probably will be sliced to the right because the club can do nothing but move well to the left of the intended directional line, drawing the club across the ball. Remember that the arms are attached to the shoulders and must go in the same direction as the shoulders. The shoulders likewise must move the same way as the hips and legs. The hips and legs are controlled by the feet.

35

Side view of a player using the correct stance—which is almost square or slightly closed. This illustrates that the body is in position to allow the swing to continue right down the direction line.

looking for accuracy, more power is a necessity. Gradually more body turn is accomplished to gain this extra power, by simply setting the feet to permit it.

HEAD POSITION

Head position will be discussed only once in this book. Still, it is one element that cannot be left out of any educational discussion on golf.

For all shots, the head must remain on its same starting axis. I think to say that the head remains absolutely still is a fallacy, for the head does rotate slightly in most swings.

One other matter to be expected during a full swing with a driver—as will be shown by some of the illustrations later in this book—is that the head remains practically still from the beginning of the backswing and during the down swing until the ball is hit. After that point, the head will move slightly forward, because of the swinging momentum set up by the movement of the body.

Too much stress cannot be placed upon the importance of good head position. It is absolutely essential to the consistent success of all types of shots. As stated before, head position will not be mentioned again because it carries the same importance in every shot. It is the gyroscope of the entire swing, so far as balance is concerned.

CHAPTER III

THE SWING

AT THIS POINT I think it is necessary to begin tying in the stance, grip, and swing. Let me reiterate that with the proper grip and stance, the proper swing is practically sure to follow.

A brief outline of the fundamentals of the swing reveals first a relatively straight left arm—though I know that in cases of middle-aged people taking up golf for the first time, it might be almost impossible to swing with a perfectly straight left arm. However, at least some semblance of this should be attempted and worked at until mastered as nearly as possible.

By means of a straight left arm, one movement—that of the elbow joint—is eliminated, and this allows the left arm to act as a fulcrum in the movement of both hands when hitting the ball. The more troublesome phases that can be eliminated from a golf swing, the more simple the process of hitting the ball correctly will become.

The next item we will consider is that of balance, which ties in directly with a proper stance. First, observe yourself walking. Are you slightly slue-footed? Are you pigeon-toed? Or do you walk with your feet pointing straight ahead?

About 90 per cent of all men are slightly slue-footed.

That is, their toes point in an outward direction normally.

Your feet should be placed in a golf swing in the same position they assume when you walk. If you walk naturally with your toes pointed slightly outward and you started to pick up a heavy weight, or to run, or to hit somebody with your fist, you surely would not assume a stance different from the one that is natural for you. If you take an unnatural stance, you are sure to lose leverage, and the result will be lack of power in your swing.

This little personal reminder of what comes naturally to you will follow through your entire golf game. For instance, if you take your stance at a golf ball and discover either foot is pointing in an unnatural directtion, correct it immediately. Otherwise you will invite trouble and almost surely come up with one of the common faults —either a slice, hook, pull, or push.

A faulty stance almost invariably will force your shoulders and the entire line of your body to cut the swing of your club across the ball.

Your ankles will bend in only one direction when standing, so to speak, and that is up and down. If you set your feet and ankles in a direction that throws your body off line, the swing of the hands and arms will naturally follow and be off line. The swing of the golf club itself is executed merely with the hands and arms and will definitely follow the pattern set up, starting with your feet.

The key to the whole solution is to set what we will call the immobile part of the body—the feet, legs, hips, and shoulders—on the proper line to your objective. Then the mobile parts—the hands and arms—which you actually think about moving, will naturally follow the correct pattern.

Item three to be considered is the plane of the swing —upright, medium, or flat. I like to imagine my swing simulating a wheel lying at about a 45-degree angle to the ground. The club, hands, and arms all go back in one definite track, which at the top of the swing points the club directly at the hole, the objective. Then it comes back down in that same track and finishes swinging at the objective.

This can be accomplished very simply if the rest of the body is properly set before the swing begins.

BALANCE AND FREEDOM OF MOVEMENT

Proper balance and freedom of movement are essential to accomplish the desired swing.

First, a definite flexing or slight bending of the knees is necessary in all shots. Try it on yourself. Stand up and take a golf stance. Then, with your knees straight back in the sockets, try to turn your body around and look behind yourself. You'll find it mighty hard to accomplish. Now bend the knees slightly, and you will find the entire body will "give" and co-ordinate quite easily.

The next item to consider in the stance is the distribution of your weight.

The weight should run from the balls of the feet back to the heels. The person who lets his weight rest on his toes is very susceptible to losing his balance and moving his head forward in the direction of the hole during the swing. This can cause many faults, the worst of all being a "shank."

A shank is a shot in which the ball is struck directly on the hosel or shaft of the club. This makes the ball fly at almost right angles to the intended line. And mind you, the ball need be hit only about an inch away from the centre of the club face to do this. However, you will find that by concentrating the weight back near the heels before the swing is even started, the head will not move forward at all.

Also in this stance, I like to feel that my weight is concentrated toward the inside of my feet. This is carried out rather simply in the swing by feeling on the backswing that the left foot rolls in toward the ball. Or you can feel that the left knee makes an inward movement toward the centre of the two feet.

On the downswing and follow-through, I like to feel my right foot and right knee roll in toward the centre of the two feet. This slight rolling movement starts, though in a very slight degree, from almost the shortest shot after the chip shot.

FIRST MOVEMENT OF THE BACKSWING

I won't attempt to say whether the body or the hands make the first movement, though I have noticed that in most good players there is a slight forward press. That means that the hands and the body—particularly the knees—seem to make a little reflex movement to the left. This simply acts to get the body out of its stable position and to start the backswing in a smooth motion instead of with a jerk.

I do not feel that a conscious effort to start either the body or the hands first is advisable, though I firmly believe a slight forward press is good. It is definitely a relaxing, tension-removing motion and seems to allow everything to start back together as a unit.

The one conscious effort that I make at the beginning of my backswing is an attempt to start the arms back without any cocking or even movement of the wrists. I like to take my hands past my right knee on the backswing before I allow any beginning of the cocking of the wrists. I can count on one hand the players that I have ever seen—good or bad—who were forced to make a conscious effort to cock the wrists. I definitely think cocking the wrists is a natural thing to do and should not be thought of once the swing is well under way.

I definitely believe the path of the arms should be considered when trying to groove the golf swing. If the arms follow the proper path, the wrists will take care of themselves. The best guide I know to a well-grooved backswing and downswing is to keep the right elbow close to the body going up and coming down. In a full drive, of course, it is impossible to get the hands above shoulder height and still keep the right elbow against the body. So the next best effort is to keep the right elbow pointing to the ground at all times. Without the elbow against the body, the backswing can go almost anywhere. It has no guide. However, with the right elbow brushing against the right side on the backswing and downswing of all shots, it becomes quite simple to swing exactly the same way every time.

One thing I advocate strongly is a firm grip with the left hand. Very few people can form less than a right angle with the shaft of the club and the left forearm at the top of the swing *if the club is held firmly in the left hand*. There are some very few exceptions—people who are extremely agile and limber. However, that right angle at the top serves as a good check. Whenever I look at the top of my swing and see the club shaft and my left forearm forming less than a 90-degree angle, I know I am not holding the club firmly enough in the last three fingers of my left hand. That is most important. Remember, too, that *the length of your swing is determined by how high you get your hands on the backswing,* not by the position of the club head.

POSTURE

In placing your club behind the ball and taking your stance, posture is extremely important. I recommend the rather erect stance, though some slight crouch cannot be prevented.

The most certain and simplest way to make sure you are standing the proper distance from the ball is to sole the bottom of the club flat on the ground and then step up to the club. With the arms fully extended but not rigid, the club itself will force you to stand correctly.

At the point of contact with the ball during the downswing, it is almost essential that both arms be practically straight. As a result, it is much simpler to start out at the address with the arms well extended and keep them that way, rather than try to correct the bending of the arms during the swing.

43

This picture shows a player attempting to take a full swing
with his knees stiff in their sockets. You will notice that this
seriously restricts the turn of the body and completely
eliminates proper co-ordination.

This shows player taking correct backswing, flexing the right knee slightly, and permitting the left knee to bend in toward the right leg. This permits a full, uninhibited swing.

Here the player is taking an incorrect, sloppy grip at the top of the backswing. By loosening the grip when his swing reaches this position, he is merely fooling himself into thinking he is taking a longer swing because the club drops below the horizontal plane at the top of the backswing.

This front view of player correctly taking the maximum full backswing shows the club in an almost horizontal position. The hands are also much higher than in the preceding illustration. The grip of both hands is still firm.

47

CHAPTER IV

CHIPPING AND PITCHING

FIRST, let's distinguish between chip shots and pitch shots.

A chip shot is one played near the green, the purpose of which is to hit the ball on to the edge of the green and let it roll to the hole.

A pitch shot is an elevated type of shot usually played with the intention of pitching the ball well on to the middle of the green—almost to the hole—and stopping it quickly. This is frequently used to shoot over obstacles.

It is my opinion that all chip shots and pitch shots should be played to carry on to the putting surface *in the air,* thereby eliminating any chance of the ball hitting some bump or depression in the turf and taking a bad " kick ".

CHIP SHOTS

The primary consideration in a chip shot is the proper selection of a club. I like to choose a club with which, without attempting to do anything but hit the ball solidly, and depending on the loft of the club, I can chip the ball about 3 to 5 feet on to the edge of the

48

green and let the remaining distance be covered by the amount of roll that the ball takes.

For instance, if my ball were lying 5 to 10 feet off the edge of the green and the flag were only 15 to 20 feet from the edge of the green, I probably would chip with a No. 8 or 9 iron. I would select the spot between my ball and the hole which is only 3 to 5 feet on the green. Then I would chip my ball on to that spot and not worry about the hole.

On the same shot, if the pin were about 40 feet from the edge of the green, I probably would take about a No. 4 or 5 iron and chip to that same spot on the green. Once again, I would depend on the greater amount of roll the less lofted club would naturally furnish to take care of the distance of my shot.

With just a minimum of practice, anyone can learn approximately how far each club will make the ball roll when chipping it on to the green.

Now, having selected the proper club and having observed the green and chosen the spot I want to chip to, the next essential item is to hit the ball solidly. Only by hitting the ball the same way every time can you possibly achieve the same amount of distance in the roll.

In a chip shot, I advocate a very open stance, with the ball played almost off the right toe and the hands well forward. The actual shot itself should be played with a minimum of wrist movement. The stroke should have a relatively short backswing, and the ball should be struck a firm blow. The body should play as little part as possible in this shot. The chip must be played almost completely with the arms and hands.

Never try to hit up on a chip shot. The ball should

D

be struck either a slight downward blow or caught just on the bottom of the arc of the swing. Remember that the loft of the club will lift the ball. Don't try to lift it yourself. That results only in a disastrous scooping motion.

Often I find it good practice to play uphill chip shots with the blade of the club slightly closed or toed in. This makes the ball roll a little farther. Downhill chip shots should be played the opposite way, with the club slightly opened up.

PITCH SHOTS

Pitch shots are played almost exclusively with a No. 8 iron, No. 9 iron, or a pitching wedge.

The swing for the pitch is almost identical to that for the chip shot, with one big exception: *The wrists are definitely cocked on the backswing of the pitch, which causes a much greater elevation of the ball.*

However, once again the hands are well forward. The body plays very little part in the shot. The pitch shot—though usually longer than the chip—is very seldom played with the maximum length of any club, thus requiring less effort in the swing and resulting in a more accurate shot.

I recommend in all chip shots and pitch shots that the hands be placed down near the middle of the grip of the club. This allows for more firmness and authority in each shot without hitting the ball too far.

In trying to stop a golf ball quickly on the green, or putting " stuff " on the ball, in the vernacular of the pro, the secret is in not trying to add a lot of hand action or other manoeuvres to the shot but in striking the ball a slight downward blow, down and through, and mainly striking the ball first on the lines in the face of the club.

The action is exactly the same as hitting a pool ball with the cue. If you try to hit a pool ball with no chalk on the cue, you usually will miscue and not get any spin at all. Likewise, a golf club will not get any spin on the ball if you hit behind the ball or get grass between the ball and the club.

The loft of the club and the lines on the face of the club will give you all the backspin you will ever need if you simply hit the ball first in the middle of the face of the club.

his is the stance for chipping with ɪy club. The arms are fully extended, ɪd the hands are slightly forward of ɪe ball. The club is held approximately ɪ the middle of the grip.

51

In the backswing for a chip shot the is practically no movement of the bod There is a very slight cocking of t wrists, but it is almost a stiff-arm sh

This picture illustrates contact with t ball during a chip shot. The arms a still extended and there is still no boc movement.

At the finish of the chip shot the arms remain extended. The club head has never passed the left hand.

This is the stance for an elevated pitch shot. The club face is slightly open. The ball is played with an open stance, and from about the centre of the two feet. The weight is evenly distributed between the feet.

53

In the backswing for a pitch shot the weight remains evenly distributed between the two feet. The wrists are definitely cocked, causing more elevation in the shot.

Just before contacting the ball on the downswing, the hands are still leading

54

ishing the swing of the pitch shot,
arms are still well extended and the
ad remains stationary.

This is the stance with a No. 9 iron.

This is the stance with a No. 8 iron

This is the stance with a No. 7 iron

This is the stance with a No. 6 iron.

This is the stance with a No. 5 iron.

57

This is the stance with a No. 4 iron.

This is the stance with a No. 3 iron.

This is the stance with a No. 2 iron.

This is the stance with either a No. 3 or a No. 4 wood.

59

This is the stance with a No. 2 wood

This is the stance with a driver.

60

CHAPTER V

INDIVIDUAL CLUBS

SINCE there are many variations in strokes with each of the irons and woods, I believe each club should be discussed separately. Some of the variations are minor and almost unnoticed by the average golfer, but they are all sound and necessary to a consistent golf game. I'll begin with the No. 9 iron and work through to the No. 2 iron. Then we'll take up the four wood clubs commonly used.

THE NO. 9 IRON

The No. 9 iron is a club recommended for use at a maximum of 100 to 110 yards. You will find it possible to hit the ball 10 to 15 yards farther with this club at times. However, I do not consider this advisable, because you then begin sacrificing accuracy for a brutal type of blow which must be considered nothing but slugging.

The minimum distance for this club could go all the way back to a foot off the green.

The No. 9 iron—whether it is used for a full shot, a three-quarter shot, or a short pitch shot—is the beginning of the swing at the golf ball.

No matter whether it be a pitch shot, a three-quarter shot, or a full shot, it fits into the wheel that I like to imagine my golf swing resembles.

The No. 9 iron requires an open stance, with the feet relatively close together—I would say 6 to 8 inches apart at the heels. In this type of swing the toes of both feet are pointed slightly outward. However, remember that because of the angle of the body with an open stance, the right foot will appear to point almost directly at the line to the hole.

The grip for the No. 9 iron is exactly the same as in all other shots except the putt. This iron is played with an open stance because it is a shot demanding a great deal of accuracy. The body is purposely eliminated from the shot as much as possible, while still allowing freedom of movement. The ball is played about off the right heel, or in general terms, somewhere between the centre of the two feet and the right foot.

All iron shots are struck a descending type of blow, *down and through the ball.* You can depend on the loft of the club 100 per cent to attain the height of flight.

I find that I enjoy the greatest success with the No. 9 iron with the weight distributed about evenly on both feet—possibly concentrated a little more on the left side.

Once again, on this shot I cannot emphasize too strongly the importance of a full extension of the arms with the left arm and the club forming approximately a straight line. This simply eliminates one more place where you might get into trouble.

Whenever attempting to hit a shorter shot with a full swing, merely hold the club farther down the grip—

"choke" it slightly. In this way, you may strike the ball a firm blow and still not realize the maximum distance that you otherwise would by holding the club at the end of the grip.

THE PITCHING WEDGE

The pitching wedge, for all practical purposes, is nothing other than about a No. 10 iron. It is simply another club to be used like the No. 9 iron, from even shorter distances and with the possibility of attaining more elevation in the flight of the ball.

The pitching wedge is used when the highest possible elevation of the ball is needed. Most golfers usually will make the common error of trying to "lift" the ball with the club to attain the extra height. As mentioned previously, this is a mistake with any club. Always depend upon the loft of the club face to propel the shot upward and carry it over whatever obstacle lies between the ball and the cup.

Hit down and through the ball, and never let the club head pass the hands on the downswing.

THE NO. 8 IRON

The No. 8 iron is a club recommended for shots 10 to 15 yards longer than the No. 9 iron—that is, about 110 to 125 yards.

The No. 8 iron is less lofted than the No. 9 and has a longer shaft. *Never forget the fact that the length of the shaft has every bit as much to do with the difference in distance as does the loft of the club.* The longer the shaft, the farther you can hit the shot. The less loft of the club, the longer you can hit the shot.

63

In the stance for a No. 9 iron shot, the ball is played approximately the same as for a pitch shot—perhaps a bit farther back toward the right heel.

At the top of the backswing with the No. 9 iron, there is a slight body turn. There is also a slight rolling of the left foot.

The finishing position of a No. 9 iron
shot shows the hands higher than the
head.

The material difference between the stances of the
No. 8 and the No. 9 irons is very slight. As we go from
the No. 9 iron back down through the No. 2 iron and
to the driver, the stance is a progression from an open
stance (with the feet very close together) and the ball
played back in the direction of the right foot to a
square or slightly closed stance with the feet the
maximum width apart (about the width of the
individual's shoulders). The ball is played more toward
the left foot with each progressing shot.

The No. 8 iron still requires the open stance—but
not quite so much so as the No. 9—and is played more
toward the centre of the feet. The feet are just slightly
wider apart, possibly not more than an inch or two.

The No. 8 iron, as a general rule, is used for a three-
quarter or full shot. Naturally, with the slight change
of stance toward the more powerful shot, the body

E   65

plays a little bigger part than it did with the No. 9 iron or the pitching wedge.

THE NO. 7 IRON

Once again, we have a little longer shot—from about 125 to 135 yards. The stance for the No. 7 iron has the same slight alteration—the feet a little wider apart, the ball played just a little back of the centre of the feet, the stance just slightly open and the swing a little fuller.

As the swing becomes longer with each progressive club, the hands reach higher on the backswing. No conscious effort need be exerted to accomplish this. The alteration of the stance allows more body turn with no more effort, and consequently the hands just automatically extend higher.

Continue to strike down and through the ball. On all iron shots, the ball should be hit first. Then the club should dig slightly into the ground, taking a divot after the ball is struck.

Often you will be faced with the problem of choosing the correct iron for a particular shot. Unless you are familiar with the maximum distance you can obtain with each club, you are apt to guess wrong and over- or undershoot the green.

I have found it is a fine idea to practise with all the irons (and woods too, for that matter) until I am fairly certain just how far I can hit each shot. Then when I'm faced with a choice of clubs, I don't have as much trouble deciding which one to use.

THE NO. 6 IRON

This club should be used from 135 yards to a maximum of 145 or 150 yards.

In the stance with a No. 7 iron, the ball is played approximately in the centre of the feet, and the posture is a little more erect.

The top of the backswing for a No. 7 iron shot is identical with that of the No. 9 iron except there is a slightly longer and fuller swing with the extra amount of body turn that the extra height of the hands will naturally cause.

The completed follow-through of the No. 7 iron shot again is slightly fuller than the No. 9 iron follow-through.

There is a very slight change from the No. 7 iron, with the stance a bit wider and more nearly square. The swing is also fuller.

Let me remind you not to hurry your backswing with the No. 6 iron—or any other club. In order to prevent a jerky movement which will ruin your entire swing, exaggerate the slowness of the backswing for a while. Then, slowly increase the speed of each backswing until you have found the tempo most comfortable to you.

Start the downswing slowly and constantly increase your speed until contact is made with the ball.

THE NO. 5 IRON

This is the middle club of the set—the halfway mark between an accuracy shot and a powerful swing.

This club probably offers more variations in its possibilities than any other club except perhaps the No. 9 iron. Because of its construction, the No. 5 iron is frequently used from 140 yards all the way up to 165 yards. It seems to be a wonderful club with which to play a variety of three-quarter shots, to hit against the wind, to play pitch-and-run shots or almost any other conceivable type of shot you may encounter.

I like to play the No. 5 iron with the ball about squarely between the feet, the stance almost square to the direction line to the hole. In some instances, I use a slightly open stance with the No. 5 iron.

You are probably wondering why, with each progressive club from the No. 9 iron toward the longer clubs, the ball is played continually more toward the left foot. There is a very definite reason, revolving around the momentum the body creates on the downswing and follow-through.

You will remember that I said that with the No. 9 iron the weight is rather evenly distributed on both feet, or slightly on the left side. However, with each increasingly longer shot and change of club, there begins a gradual shifting of the weight from both feet at the address of the ball slightly to the right side at the top of the backswing. Then with the downward swing of the arms and clubs, the body naturally begins to shift back to the left side.

It is almost the same principle every good hitter in baseball employs when he rears back and leans into a pitch. The shift of the weight is exactly the same, except both feet stay in the same place in the golf swing.

For a No. 5 iron shot the ball is played from midway between the two feet, with the arms well extended.

At the top of the backswing with the No. 5 iron, the angle formed by the club and the left forearm is almost a right angle. This is true of all the preceding and following backswing pictures.

In this completed follow-through with the No. 5 iron, notice the turned-over position of the left foot. This is caused by the increasing momentum of the longer shots. Although I do not advocate turning the left foot in such a manner, many people (including myself) cannot prevent it.

THE NO. 4 IRON

We are now getting into the long artillery class of iron clubs. Though we never can forget that accuracy is a prime objective in all shots, we now are slowly leaving that type of swing and moving into the full-turn, full-swing type of shot.

The No. 4 iron is a club used for ordinary purposes from 160 to 170 or 175 yards. The ball now is played slightly past centre in the direction of the left heel. The stance is wider, almost the width of the shoulders, and is square to the direction line.

Now the swing becomes a combination of arm and body turn, which, let me emphasize again, is accomplished by the proper stance and not by any conscious effort. The hands are now shoulder-high or slightly higher at the top of the backswing. The club still strikes the ball a descending blow, down and through the ball, depending on the loft of the club to elevate the ball.

I have a little habit I now use in the longer irons, but it also is just as valuable in short shots. Before addressing the ball, I like to pick out a spot on the grass 3 or 4 inches in front of the ball, exactly in line between the ball and the flag toward which I am shooting. Then, on my downswing, I think of driving the ball into the ground and right through that imaginary spot I have picked out.

By doing this, you can rather easily eliminate one of the greatest faults in golf—" quitting " on the shot, or slapping at the ball with no particular thought of driving it right down a line or path in the direction of the flag.

THE NO. 3 IRON

This club should be used for shots from 170 to 185 yards. The stance is slightly wider than for the No. 4 iron, still about square. The ball is played slightly more toward the left heel, and a slightly fuller swing is required.

Remember, in all shots that increase in length from the No. 9 iron on up to the driver, you should stand slightly farther away from the ball. This should be done because the shafts are increasingly longer. It is no problem to do this if you will remember (as was mentioned earlier) the little gimmick of soling the club flat on the ground behind the ball and then merely stepping to the club, with the arms fully extended but not rigid.

No iron shot should be swept cleanly off the turf without taking a divot. The ideal shot will dig up a spot just in front of the ball's position. This proves the ball was hit a downward stroke. Kindly remember to replace the turf.

If the ground is dug up just behind the ball's position, you know you are striking the ball on the upward swing or dipping your head and diving at it. In committing this error, you are failing to hit the ball with the full force of your swing. The swing has lost some of its momentum in striking the ball after it has struck the ground.

THE NO. 2 IRON

This is the club scheduled for distances up to 200

1 this stance for a No. 3 iron shot, ou will notice that the width of the tance is increasing as the longer irons re used. The ball is also played slightly 1ore forward toward the left foot, be- ause of the momentum.

73

The club is now in an almost horizonta position at the top of the backswing o a No. 3 iron shot.

The complete follow-through of th No. 3 iron swing shows the club pointin; toward you readers. This is caused b what you might call a recoil action i stopping the terrific speed set up by th club head and shoulders in the swing

yards. You are now dealing with the big gun of the iron set.

I have heard many professionals and amateurs claim the No. 2 iron is the hardest club in the set to use. I do not believe this is necessarily true. When you attempt to play this shot, get the fact firmly entrenched in your mind that to hit it well you must think primarily of hitting the ball solidly with a smooth swing. *Above all, do not attempt to force extra distance out of this club.*

Follow these principles, and you will not have much difficulty in hitting a No. 2 iron.

You have the amount of loft and the length of shaft in a No. 2 iron that will give you about a 200-yard shot with no more conscious effort than you required in hitting the No. 5 iron 160 yards.

The stance with the No. 2 iron is almost maximum width. The ball is played almost to the left heel, and once again, do not let the lack of loft of the club scare you. Strike down and through the ball, trying to make your club swing right at your target as nearly as possible.

I prefer a slightly closed stance with this club, although there is no absolutely concrete rule on this. Either a square stance or a very slightly open one is just as good, depending on which is most comfortable to the individual.

THE NO. 4 WOOD

By necessity, the No. 4 wood and the No. 2 iron must be tied closely together. The distance for the two clubs does not vary greatly, though it is possible at times to hit a shot with a No. 4 wood a good deal farther than with a No. 2 iron.

75

However, the two clubs tie in together in this way. If you are the least bit in doubt that your shot can reach the green when hit with your No. 2 iron, then choose the No. 4 wood. That is why, all the way through the set, you have a progression of clubs that, for general purposes, are only about 10 yards apart in their maximum distances.

I like to play the No. 4 wood just inside the left heel. It is a fine club for playing the ball from relatively bad lies or close lies where the ball sits down in the grass so that it is almost impossible to hit a very good shot with the No. 2 iron, because of the structure of the club head.

The swing with the No. 4 wood is no different from that of the No. 2 iron, except that you might possibly use a little longer swing if you really want to " bust " it.

You can conduct your own little experiment with these two clubs. Hold the No. 2 iron at the end of the shaft and hit a nice, full shot. Then choke the No. 4 wood about 2 or 3 inches down the shaft and hit a full shot. You will discover that the distances of the two shots will be almost the same.

So you actually have no gap in distance between the clubs—and the selection of your club is mostly a matter of choice determined by lie, wind, etc.

The No. 4 wood is also the intermediate point between hitting the ball a downward blow and merely catching the ball at the bottom of the arc and sweeping it off the grass. If the lie looks a little too close or down in a hole, I advise at all times striking the ball a downward blow—exactly the same as with the irons. However, if the ball is sitting up nicely, then play the

76

ball slightly forward toward the left foot and merely sweep it off the top of the grass.

THE NO. 3 WOOD

The No. 3 wood is a club which is played from about 210 or 215 yards up to 225 yards. Here's the club that gets the majority of my fairway play with woods. It does not require an absolutely perfect lie, although, of course, it can be played better from a good lie.

I like to play the ball about off the left heel with an absolutely square stance, and in most cases, sweep the ball right off the grass. Or, if the distance is such that you cannot reach the green with a No. 4 wood, you can use this club and still strike the ball a slightly downward blow while gaining your maximum distance.

This is assuming, of course, that you are confronted with a rather close lie, which requires this type of swing.

THE NO. 2 WOOD, OR BRASSIE

Moving on up among the woods, we reach the No. 2 wood, or brassie.

This is a club played from 225 yards up to as far as you can hit it. It is a rather dangerous club if you attempt to use it from any other than an excellent lie.

In the first place, if you don't have a good lie, you won't knock the ball any farther than you would with a spoon. In the second place, most people try to hit the ball too far with a brassie. This, once again, is a club to be used with a good, full swing and *with no attempt to hit the ball farther than you are capable of knocking it the biggest percentage of the time.*

77

I play the brassie almost exactly the same as I play the driver—right off my left heel or between the heel and left instep with a maximum stance, which is about the width of my shoulders. Then I take a full swing as with a driver.

My stance is slightly closed, both feet still pointing outward. I try to imagine I am swinging to either a little musical tune or some little jingle that will give me a definite rhythm in the swing.

I do not necessarily attempt to attain any great accuracy. *You will be much more accurate with this, and all other woods, by being sure to take a full and well-completed swing in the general direction of your objective, than trying to steer the ball down an exact line.*

THE DRIVER

The driver is at least the second most important club in the bag—the putter being the first. Driving and putting comprise about 70 per cent of golf, in my opinion. The old saying that you drive for fun and putt for money is considerably exaggerated.

There is no other shot in golf that makes a par-four or par-five hole so simple as a long, straight drive. Of course, it is necessary to possess mastery of the other shots, but a person should depend more on consistency from his driver than from any other club in his bag.

Just consider the driver for a moment. The driver is the one club in the bag for which you have the benefit of the combination of a perfectly teed-up, flat lie with a level stance every time.

In my case, I know the improvement I have

experienced in my golf game over the past five years can be attributed mostly to improved driving. In my pre-war amateur days, I was as poor a driver as any competing amateur in the country. I always obtained better than average distance in the length of my shots. However, you must remember that the long-ball hitter can go farther off line than a player who is equally wild but doesn't drive quite so far.

Just before the war and shortly thereafter, when I began to branch out from my own neighbourhood clubs and play on golf courses which placed a premium on driving, it dawned on me that I could never be any better unless I mastered that first shot which occurs on every hole (except a par-three).

The one means by which I finally realized some definite progress was by trial and error—finding out from which one of several stances I hit the greatest percentage of straight drives. Then I discovered that the very slightest variation from that stance produced rather widely different results.

Now every time I step to the tee to drive, I try to take as nearly the same stance as is humanly possible.

I attempt to have my feet at the heels the same width as my shoulders—no wider and no closer together. I attempt to have the toes of both feet pointing outward in almost exactly the same direction they point when I walk. My stance is slightly closed, my right foot being about an inch farther from the direction line on which I am attempting to hit, than is the left foot.

I play the ball almost squarely between the left heel and the left instep. I have my arms fully extended without being rigid, and there is a definite flexing or bending of the knees.

Sometimes it is rather difficult to check yourself as to whether you are lined up properly down the fairway. I frequently do this on the practice tee by taking my stance and then laying the club down, on the same line the ball is supposed to follow, so that it touches the toes of both feet. Then I look down the shaft of the club. If I am properly lined up, the club will be pointing slightly to the right centre of the fairway.

An excellent way to obtain the correct position of the feet to the ball is to first take a stance at right angles to the line along which you intend to shoot. With the heels of the feet touching, line the ball up directly between the two feet. Then, merely take a step sideways with the right foot, and you will be in perfect position.

As much golf as I play, day in and day out, the stance never has become what I would call automatic. I must constantly check on it.

Now with the grip established on the club, before even approaching the ball and taking what I think is the correct stance, I like to concentrate on one item— smoothness in my swing.

Once again let me remind you to take the club back in one piece. That is, don't move the wrists or hands in any way until the club has passed the right knee. Remember the inward movement of the left knee and the rolling of the left foot in toward the centre of the feet. This movement occurs at the start of the backswing.

Keep the right elbow relatively close to the right side, get your hands more than shoulder-high while still keeping a fairly straight left arm, and be sure the right elbow continues to point at the ground. Those are the points to remember as the club goes back.

After having mastered a good backswing, the down-swing is almost automatic. I like to think of having the club head continually increase its speed, faster and faster, not until I am just *at* the ball, but several feet beyond it. I like to think of that little imaginary spot about six inches in front of my ball, right on the line in which I want the ball to start. After I once start my downswing, I definitely want no other thought to inhibit my freedom and speed of swing.

It boils down to this. A player can take pains and time in getting his grip and stance correct and still not suffer any tension or loss of concentration. Then, assuming our other principles of a good swing have been practised enough so they have become fairly automatic, think of nothing but smoothness of swing and club head speed through the ball and on the line of flight as far as your arms and shoulders will allow the club to swing.

THE DRIVER AND THE SWING

The swing with the driver is the sum total of all the swings with other clubs. May I say again, I think *the general arc of the swing with each club is the same (so far as it goes) as the swing with the driver.* The full swing with the driver embraces all the other swings and is an extension of them to the farthest point the human body permits. In other words, it is the completed physiology of the golf game.

In the practice of developing a golf swing and

F   81

mastering its intricacies, too much time cannot be devoted to chipping and putting. However, for the actual grooving of the swing itself, I think practice with the driver—after the preliminary limbering up—is much better than practice with the middle irons. Practice with the driver creates a much fuller and more rhythmic swing, whereas continued practice with the middle irons will almost invariably tend to make your swing short, and sometimes too punchy or too jerky.

When you have developed a full, smooth swing with which you can drive consistently well, the other portions of the game, all the way back to the chip shots, are merely a problem of adjusting your stance and address to the ball to force you to use that portion of the swing which is necessary.

For those of you who don't have the opportunity to play more than week-end golf, I think practice in front of a mirror is excellent. From the pictures in this book, you can compare your swing with mine. I never would go so far as to say my swing is perfect. However, I sincerely try to follow the fundamentals of golf which are considered absolutely essential to good play.

There is one musical recording I think is excellent for practising a golf swing. That is the " Merry Widow Waltz ". There is just the right tempo in that particular piece of music so that a smooth golf swing can be patterned almost perfectly with it. There probably are many others, but that one I especially recommend.

ance for the drive. The ball is played
st inside the left heel. The feet are
bout as far apart as the width of the
houlders, the knees are flexed, the
ody is erect and the arms are fully ex-
nded. The line of the left arm and
ub is almost straight. The weight is
bout equally divided.

tarting back. Notice that the move-
nent of the club, the arms, and the
pper body is all in one piece. There is
o break in the wrists. The hips haven't
urned as much as the shoulders but the
veight already has moved largely to the
ight leg. Notice also that there has
een no rolling of the wrists.

Only now are the wrists beginning t
break or " cock " when the left arm
about parallel to the ground. More
the weight has moved to the right le
Both hips and shoulders have turne
with the shoulders still leading. Th
left arm is straight.

Near the top. The body is coilin
almost to its limit. The weight is almos
entirely on the right leg, with only th
inside of the ball of the left foot carry
ing any pressure. The hips have turne
almost 90 degrees, the shoulders mor
that 90 degrees. The left arm is straigh
and the grip tight.

At the top—in perfect form. The wind-up is complete here, with the weight nearly all on the right leg, hips and shoulders fully turned, the left arm straight, the grip firm with both hands, and the club dipping every so slightly below the horizontal.

Starting the downswing. Here is the first movement towards the ball, and if you look closely you will see that it is made with the hips. The hips, the left leg, and the left foot are the only things that have changed much from the preceding picture. The hips are turning back towards the ball, the weight is moving back to the left, and the left leg is coming back into position to support it. The left heel is almost back on the ground again. Yet the hands have scarcely moved.

Two-thirds of the way down. The cl[ub]
is going into the hitting area now, a[nd]
there are three important points [to]
notice. One is the transfer of weig[ht]
back to the braced left leg with [the]
flexed knee. The hips are leading t[he]
shift of weight and are getting "out [of]
the way" of the hands and right ar[m.]
The second point is the hugging of t[he]
body by the right arm, with the rig[ht]
elbow in close. Third is the action [of]
the shoulders. Notice that they have[n't]
turned nearly so much as the hips a[nd]
that the right shoulder is going dow[n]
rather than around.

Just before contact. All the points [in]
the previous picture are shown mo[re]
sharply here. The weight is so far ov[er]
on the left leg that the right heel h[as]
risen. The right elbow is still close, a[nd]
the right shoulder is still going dow[n.]
Note how much farther the hips ha[ve]
turned than the shoulders. The b[ig]
difference here is that the wrist "coc[k"]
is almost discharged.

through the ball. The main points in the two previous pictures are still more sharply defined. The weight is so far to the left that the left foot is rolling to the outside. The shoulders have turned more but it is clear that the right shoulder is dropping; note its position compared with the left shoulder. The wrist " cock " was discharged completely just as the ball was hit.

The ball is well on its way now and the head is beginning to move. The right shoulder is coming down and through, the right hand has climbed over the left, and the weight is so far to the left that only the toe of the right foot is touching the ground. Note again how the whole mid-portion of the body is " out of the way."

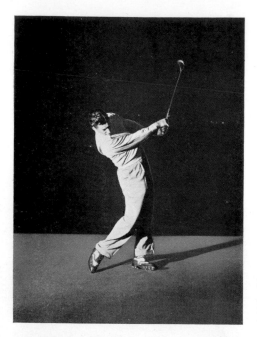

All the work is done now and t[he]
body is beginning to relax. The weig[ht]
is supported by only the outside of t[he]
left foot and the toe of the right.

The shot is made, the follow-through
complete, and the eyes can follow t[he]
ball. The height of the hands at the fi[n]
ish reveals that the wrist " cock " w[as]
discharged late, as it should be. The[re]
was no " quitting " on this shot.

CHAPTER VI

TRAP SHOTS

THIS probably will come as a revolting development to you who have religiously studied the first part of this book. However, at one time or another you are sure to press the wrong button and end up in the average golfer's most dreaded territory—the clammy, white sand trap with those ugly jutting jaws which frequently grab a perfectly hit shot as well as the bad ones.

The sand·trap shot does not differ from the normal shot in the actual swing, although it does vary in its method of sending the ball on its way. Whereas with the normal iron shot you attempt to strike the ball first, with the semi-explosion shot from a sand trap—which I use at all times within 20 yards of the flag—the object is *never* to strike the ball first.

The first objective for any player approaching a sand shot is getting out of the trap. Great accuracy definitely can be expected from a master sand player; still, even the best players realize that getting out of the trap and on to the putting surface is a very satisfactory result in itself.

TECHNIQUE OF THE SHOT

A semi-explosion or explosion shot, played with a

sand wedge, never allows the club to touch the ball. I have a rather short-shafted sand wedge which I grip exactly on the end of the club every time from a normal lie in a sand trap. If you choose to hold the club farther down the grip, the one essential thing is to hold it in exactly the same place every time.

I take a stance about as wide as that which I use on my No. 2 or No. 3 iron. I definitely attempt to stand exactly the same way every time and play the ball off my left heel. I take a slightly open stance because my actual swing is a little bit more upright—and from the outside in. Then I cut very slightly across the line to the flag with my swing. The swing is like a lazy, loose practice swing, not a hard one.

After taking the correct stance and grip, the next thing is to be sure the club face is as wide open as possible. In other words, the club should be turned back so that it has more loft than normal. With this open position of the club, the flange or sole on the bottom of the club is set at such an angle that it will not dig deeply into the sand but will hit the sand and almost bounce.

If your ball is buried, of course, you will have to close the face of the club enough so that you're sure of digging deeply enough to blast the ball out of its position and up on to the green.

During the swing proper, I concentrate my weight on the left side. By doing this I have a better chance of striking the sand with the club exactly at the spot I desire.

Having taken a stance and a grip—the grip being the same as in all other golf shots except putting—we are now ready to begin the shot. I try to hit approximately the same distance behind the ball every time, which is about 3 or 4 inches, and hit a little harder on longer shots.

Finally, the other part of the shot which cannot be neglected is the follow-through. The follow-through is the one item which will assure you of getting out of that sand trap.

For a buried lie, I play the shot exactly the same as for an unburied one, except that then I close the face of the club, or toe the club in. By this means, the angle of the flange on the bottom of the club is such that it digs sharply into the sand and once again gets under the ball.

This, together with the follow-through, brings the ball up and out. It is impossible to prevent a buried trap shot from rolling after it hits the ground. The other shot, the semi-explosion from a good lie in the trap, will invariably have a good deal of backspin. They must be played accordingly.

UPHILL AND DOWNHILL LIES IN SANDTRAPS

I have discovered that the best way of playing side-hill trap shots is by taking my stance in the trap and sinking one foot or the other farther into the sand until I come as close as possible to having a normal, flat stance. Then I merely play the shot the same way as if the lie were flat. With an uphill lie, sink the left foot deeper in the sand than the right one; with a downhill lie, just the opposite.

CHIP SHOTS FROM SAND TRAPS

Chip shots are, for the most part, to be avoided from sand traps. The first necessary prerequisite for a chip shot in a trap is a perfect lie, with the ball sitting high and almost out of the sand. The next absolutely necessary element is not to hit behind the ball. Even half topping the chip shot out of the sand is much, much better than hitting the slightest fraction of an inch behind it. If you have ever tried this precarious shot, you know that hitting the least bit behind the ball will leave it in the trap.

I never try a chip shot from any sand trap which has a bank more than 1 to 2 feet high. As a matter of fact, I never chip out of sand traps bordering the green.

The one time chip shots out of a sand trap are recommended is when a trap lies 20 to 30 yards or more from the green. Then you actually get into the pitch-shot class. However, once again, the prime requisite is to hit the ball first.

When I do find it necessary to chip from a trap, I plant my feet firmly in the sand with the same stance I use on any chip shot around the green. Next, I make it a definite point to stand a little more upright and to extend my arms to the fullest without being too rigid. Then I try to eliminate all body movement from the shot, and merely hit it with my hands and arms—striking slightly downward and hitting the ball first.

The selection of the club to be used to chip out of a trap doesn't make too much difference, as long as you can clear the edge of the trap. However, I never would use a sand wedge, a pitching wedge, or even a No. 9 iron when chipping from a sand trap.

This picture shows the proper address for a trap shot from a normal, unburied lie. Notice that the feet are planted firmly in the trap, and the club face is extremely open.

Now we see the same address, but the ball here is partly buried. The feet are once again sunk down into the sand for a solid base. The only difference between this shot and a normal, un-buried trap shot is that here the club face is closed so that it will dig readily into the sand. The rest of the stroke is the same.

At the halfway point in the backswing, note that the head and general axis of the body are still anchored at the same spot. The left arm is straight, while the left knee is bent slightly, and the right leg is supporting most of the weight.

The weight has shifted to the right leg at the top of the backswing, but the head has not moved.

Halfway down the backswing, you will notice that the hands are leading and the club face is wide open. The weight has come back to the left side, the right shoulder is coming down, rather than around, while the head remains motionless.

At the point of contact, with the ball barely in front of the club face, the head remains stationary while the hands and arms continue their arc. The right shoulder is still coming down, as it must in all shots.

At this point in the swing, the club has passed the ball. The ball is coming up and out on a very lazy and slow flight towards the green. Hitting behind the ball has resulted in the blasting of the sand, according to proper technique. The right shoulder is well down now.

With the follow-through half completed, the head remains down and the face of the club is still open.

CHAPTER VII

TROUBLESOME LIES

EVEN IF you are fortunate enough to avoid the sand traps that dot the golf course, you can still be faced with troublesome shots in the middle of the fairway. Many of these difficult shots must be played from sidehill, uphill, or downhill lies.

SIDEHILL POSITION—DOWNHILL LIE

The most important phase in playing this type of shot is appreciating the fact that you must stand closer to the ball and hold the club at the end of the grip. You should also be positive that the weight is well back on the heels, so as not to lose balance by tipping forward.

The general tendency in this shot is to slice the ball, because of the position of the body. As a result, I advise aiming a little to the left of your objective and toeing the club in, or closing the blade slightly. This will overcome the tendency to slice.

SIDEHILL POSITION WITH THE BALL ABOVE THE FEET

Here it becomes necessary to " choke up " slightly on the grip of the club and to stand with the feet much farther away from the ball than is normal. The swing

G   97

for an exaggerated lie of this type becomes almost a baseball swing, and the tendency is to hook and pull the ball.

I advise playing this shot by aiming to the right of your objective and leaving the face of the club slightly open, or facing it to the right of the line to the objective. The weight must necessarily be concentrated on the balls of the feet and toes so as not to fall backward, away from the ball.

On both shots I recommend that the ball be played about in the centre of the two feet.

UPHILL LIES

In the case of an uphill lie, the ball should be played a little more forward, toward the left foot, than is normal. The weight should be slightly to the left (forward) to prevent falling away from the shot.

Also, on an uphill shot, it is logical to assume that you should use a little more club than normal because, first, you cannot take as full a swing, and second, some distance will be lost in the excess altitude your shot will take because of the upward position from which it starts.

DOWNHILL LIES

When you find yourself faced with a shot from a downhill lie, the weight should be concentrated slightly on the right side. Your main problem here is in making yourself feel balanced before starting the shot.

The ball should be played well back toward the right foot, regardless of the club you are using. It is also logical to assume you should use a little less club because

Cary receives the coveted National Open trophy from Field-ing Wallace, president of the United States Golf Association.

the trajectory of the ball will be lower, because of the downward starting position.

On a downhill shot, I like to face a little to the right of my objective and close the face of the club, to overcome the natural tendency to slice this shot. In this way I seem to be able to get a little stronger blow at the ball, though sometimes it actually causes a slight hook. But facing to the right of my objective will compensate for it.

PLAYING FROM THE ROUGH

When playing any type of shot out of high grass, the first thing that should be considered is the necessity of getting the ball up and out of the grass quickly. This cannot be accomplished merely with power.

Sam Snead, in his strongest moments, never drove a golf ball through a long patch of heavy grass by brute strength. Still, good distance can be obtained from some rather shoddy-looking lies by either of two means: first, by taking a rather well-lofted club; or secondly, by taking a club without too much loft, opening the club face and facing slightly to the left of the desired objective.

If you use a club without too much loft and open the club face, it is better to take a more upright swing —almost an outside-in type of stroke—which will pick the ball up and move it out of the grass quickly.

However, from extremely long, tough, heavily matted grass, no human being can hit the ball more than 75 to 125 or 130 yards. And if you don't use a well-lofted club, you frequently won't get out at all.

In very sparse, thin grass not more than 3 or 4

The author, Dr. Cary Middlecoff, United States Open Golf champion of 1949.

inches high, play the shot exactly as you would if it were in the fairway.

CLOSE LIES, OR BALL LYING IN A SLIGHT DEPRESSION

Close lies—in the grass or on bare ground—can be overcome very simply by just playing the ball farther back toward the right foot and striking definitely down on the ball.

Always remember: *every club in the bag has some degree of loft built into it, and if the ball is hit squarely, it will always get up into the air.* There is never an occasion to strike up or try to lift a golf shot. Depend on the loft of the club to take care of that job for you.

CHAPTER VIII

THE MENTAL SIDE

No MATTER how much physical skill you may attain in mastering the various golf shots, if you do not learn how to apply that skill, you never will be able to defeat many people who are in your class as shot makers. The skilful golfer who fails to take advantage of his skill is every bit as badly off as the person who has a well-co-ordinated body but doesn't know how to utilize it.

Your first consideration in sizing up your own golf game should come in knowing your limitations as far as distance is concerned. If you discover that your average drive—when hit well—is about 200 yards, then you cannot expect to use the same iron clubs as a person who drives 250 yards.

Let's assume you have taken stock of the amount of power you possess. Then, for illustration, let's say that you come to a par-four hole approximately 425 yards long. You know for sure your chances of getting on that green are only about one out of ten with your two best shots, so you should not attempt the impossible!

Face the facts! Hit your two best shots—not necessarily with the idea of getting on the green in two, but with the idea of playing those shots well within yourself and trying to hit them solidly. Then, more

often than not, you will have a short putt, after your
chip shot, for your par four.

Frequently, by trying to stretch your shots, you will
get into a position far off to either side from which it
is almost impossible to salvage a five.

In the National Open of 1949 on the 599-yard tenth
hole at the Medinah Country Club in Chicago, I had
not been closer than 50 yards to that green in two—
either in practice rounds or the tournament.

In the third round, with a slight following wind, I
hit a good drive. Walking down the fairway, my
thoughts were almost a prayer that I could catch a good
enough lie so that I might attempt to hit another driver
shot from the fairway and get on the green in two. This
actually was very bad thinking on my part, because the
green is well trapped on the right and unplayable to
the left.

As luck would have it, I did not have a good enough
lie to use a driver, or even a brassie. So I was forced
to take the No. 3 wood. Then, with nothing more in
mind than an attempt to put the ball in front of the
green, I hit a nice, solid No. 3 wood shot. To my utter
amazement, I found the ball on the green 15 feet from
the hole.

That was a wonderful lesson to me—that frequently
your very longest and best shots are the ones you
approach merely with a nice smooth swing, attempting
to accomplish nothing more than just to hit the ball
solidly and squarely.

I do not advocate playing " pat ball " with any golf
shots. However, I surely recommend keeping the swing
within the bounds of good balance.

In my own case, I believe my weight gradually

shifts from both feet slightly to my right side on the backswing, and then shifts back again to both feet and to the left side on the follow-through.

I believe that if you observe this one little rule of balance, you never will swing so hard at a ball that you will slip over into the slugging class.

SELECTION OF CLUBS

You can figure that from the No. 9 iron all the way through the driver, there is an average of only 10 to 15 yards difference in each succeeding club.

Whenever you are standing on the fairway, preparing to choose a club for a shot to the green—*and I do think you should depend upon yourself and not upon your caddie for the selection*—your first consideration should be that the average green is from 20 to 35 yards from front to back. If you are debating between a No. 4 iron and a No. 5 iron- -selecting as your objective the very middle of the green- remember that a shot hit perfectly with either club still will reach the putting surface of that green.

Keep in mind also that a shot hit half-heartedly— which is caused by indecision 90 per cent of the time— will not reach the green with either club.

Positive thoughts are most essential in golf. Regardless of the club you select, before starting to address the ball, decide what you are going to try to accomplish with that club. Whether you are making a full shot or a half shot, simply step up to the ball, take your stance, and swing away.

By adopting this procedure, you will eliminate practically all of the tension that mounts in your body

The new Open champion and his wife pose for photographers.

when you stand over the ball waggling the club, not knowing what you want to do.

PROCEDURE

In mentioning procedure, I have in mind one definite way to approach every shot. My own procedure has been developed from a little count I established myself. After looking over the shot and making up my mind what club to use and how I will try to hit the ball, I establish my grip on the club. Then I start my count.

On the count of one, I sole the club behind the ball. On the count of two, I place my right foot in position. On the count of three, I place my left foot in position. On the count of four, if any slight alteration is needed, I make the change. Then I waggle the club twice and fire.

In addition to helping to groove your swing and eliminating tension, this automatic procedure, plus a little routine thought about your shot, will change golf from drudgery and hard work into a real pleasure for you.

I speak from experience, because I consider my first year and a half as a golf professional on the tournament circuit as the hardest work I ever did in my life. In the past year and a half, however, after having developed both an attitude and a method of going about my work, golf once again has become a game of pleasure to me—even though it is my means of making a living.

THE AUTHOR'S TOURNAMENT RECORD

CARY MIDDLECOFF

Was born January 6, 1921, at Halls, Tennessee; is 6 ft. 2 in. tall and weighs 13 stone 3 lbs.

He has been a Golf professional since March 13, 1947; his lowest competitive score, 64, was made March 18, 1947, at Myers Park C.C.

His lowest 72-hole score is 262 which was made in 1949 at Greenbrier C.C.

RECORD

1937   Winner, Tennessee State High School Tournament.

1938   Winner, Memphis City Championship.
Qualified for American National Amateur
Tournament sectionally.

1939   Winner, Memphis City Championship.

1940   Winner, Tennessee State Championship.
Winner, West Kentucky Open Championship.
Runner-up, Southern Intercollegiate.
Quarter-finals, National Intercollegiate.
Qualified for American National Amateur, beaten by
Fred Haas, Jr., in first round.

1941   Winner, Tennessee State Championship.
Winner, West Kentucky Open.
Winner, Southeast Intercollegiate.
Quarter-finals, National Collegiate Championship.
Winner, Meridian-Mississippi Invitational.
Winner, Galloway and Pine Hills Invitational.

1942   Winner, Tennessee State Championship.

1943   Winner, Tennessee State Championship.

1945   Low amateur, Richmond Open.
Winner, North and South Open, 280, the only amateur
to ever win that tournament.

1946   Twelfth, Masters' Tournament, 292, Low amateur.
Quarter-finalist, National Amateur.

1947   Winner, Charlotte Open, in play-off with George
Schoux, 277—$2,000.
Tied sixth, Colonial Invitational, 284—$700.
Fifth, Inverness, with Sam Snead, minus 2—$450.
Tied tenth, Esmeralda Open, 281—$325.
Tied ninth, Reno Open, 280—$407.16.
Tied sixth, Denver Open, 284—$750.
Tied eighth, Atlanta Open, 287—$400.
Twenty-second Money Winner—$6,119.96.

1948   Tied seventh, Bing Crosby Tournament, 217—$225.
Fourth, Texas Open, 271—$800.
Tied sixth, Rio Grande Open, 273—$550.
Sixth, New Orleans Open, 283—$600.
Seventh, St. Petersburg Open, 280—$500.
Winner, Miami Four Ball, with Jim Ferrier, 1 up—
$1,250.
Runner-up, Charlotte Open, 274—$1,400.
Runner-up, Masters' Tournament, 284—$1,500.
Tied fifth, National Capital Open, 282—$750.
Fifth, Inverness Four-Ball partnered with Jim Ferrier,
minus 5—$450.

Seventh, Motor City Open, 280—$800.

Ninth, Columbus Open, 277—$390.

Tied ninth, Dapper Dan Open, 288—$570.

Fifth, World's Championship (Tam O'Shanter), 137.

Tied third, Denver Open, 274—$990.

Tied third, Utah Open, 277—$990.

Tied second, Tacoma Open, 274—$1,070. Participated in play-off of five-way tie for title with Ed Oliver, Fred Haas, Jr., Charles Congdon, and Vic Ghezzi. Defeated on 19th hole by Ed Oliver.

Fifth, Portland Open, 273—$900.

Fourth, Glendale Open, 283—$1,100.

Winner, Hawaiian Open, 274—$2,000.

Seventh Money Winner—$14,621.25.

1949   Tied eleventh, Los Angeles Open, 292—$423.33.

Fifth, Bing Crosby Pro-Am., teamed with Frank Stranahan, 201—$100.

Tied eighth, Bing Crosby Individual, 216—$150.

Tied third, Phoenix Open, 280—$833.33.

Runner-up, Houston Open, 273—$1,400.

Winner, Rio Grande Valley Open, 267—$2,000.

Runner-up, St. Petersburg Open 276—$1,400.

Winner, Miami Four-Ball, teamed with Jim Ferrier—$1,250.

Tied fourth, Seminole Pro-Am., 129—$550, teamed with C. Amory.

Tied third, Seminole Individual, 139—$550.

Winner, Jacksonville Open, 274—$2,000.

Tied third, Cavalier Specialists' Invitational, 202—$900.

Tied second, Wilmington Open Invitational, 278—$975.

Winner, Greenbrier Individual, 265—$1,200.

Fifth, Goodall Round Robin, plus 27—$1,000.

Tied ninth, *Philadelphia Inquirer* Open, 289—$540.

Winner, United States Open, 286—$2,000.

Co-winner, Motor City Open, 273—$2,250. Tied with

Lloyd Mangrum after 11-hole play-off. Agreed to share title.

Runner-up, *Washington Star* Open, 274—$1,900.

Winner, Reading Open, 266—$2,600.

Tied third, Dapper Dan Open, 279—$1,275.

Seventh, Inverness Four-Ball, teamed with Jim Ferrier, minus 7—$550.

Runner-up, Western Open, 272—$1,900.

Tied fourth, World's Championship of Golf, 278—$2,500.

Third, Havana Pro Individual, 275—$700.

Tied third, Kansas City Open, 285—$550.

Second Money Winner—$24,604.57.

1950 Tied ninth, Bing Crosby Pro Individual, 220—$133.33.

Tied third, Long Beach Open, 274—$900.

Tied third, Tucson Open, 270—$900.

Fourth, Texas Open, 270—$800.

Winner, Houston Open, 277—$2,000.

Tied first, Seminole Pro-Am., teamed with C. D. Dillon, 128—$1,250.

Winner, Seminole Pro Individual, 207—$1,500.

Winner, Jacksonville Open, 279—$2,000.

Tied third, Aiken Pro-Am., 62—$339.20.

Tied second, Aiken Pro Individual, 67—$210.

Tied third, Wilmington Open, 283—$900.

Tied seventh, Masters', 292—$405.

Fourth, Western Open, 284—$1,150.

Tied fifth, Colonial Invitational, 283—$850.

Tied fifth, Ft. Wayne Open, 279—$900.

Tied tenth, U.S. Open, 292—$225.

Sixth, Goodall Round Robin, plus 10—$900.

Tied ninth, Motor City Open, 282—$570.

Sixth, Inverness Round Robin, teamed with Lloyd Mangrum, minus 4—$600.

Tied twelfth, World Championship of Golf, 287—$1,250.

Fourth, Eastern Open, 283—$1,150.

Winner, St. Louis Open, 270—$2,600. Defeated Oliver in play-off on 20th hole.

Tied eleventh, Kansas City Open, 284—$423.33.

Tenth, Miami Open, 274—$340.

Semi-finalist, Miami Four-Ball, teamed with Ed Oliver —$400.

Winner, Decatur Open, 132—$500.

Sixth Money Winner—$18,205.04.

1951 Tied fourth, Los Angeles Open, 288—$1,033.33.

Second, Bing Crosby Tournament, 212—$1,250.

Winner, Lakewood Open, 271—$2,000.

Tied ninth, Phoenix Open, 278—$343.33.

Tied thirteenth, Tucson Open, 276—$195.

Tied eighth, Miami Beach Open, 280—$308.

Tied eleventh, Seminole Invitational, 214—$212.

Winner, Colonial Invitational, 282—$3,000.

Fifth, Palm Beach Tournament, plus 15—$1,000.

Tied third, Inverness, with Lloyd Mangrum, plus 3— $825.

Runner-up, Western Open, 271—$1,400.

Tied fourth, St. Paul Open, 269—$1,050.

Winner, Tam O'Shanter All American, 274—$2,250.

Seventh, Tam O'Shanter World Championship, 279— $1,800.

Tied eleventh, Sioux City Open, 270—$340.

Runner-up, Fort Wayne Open, 270—$1,800.

Winner, Eastern Open, 279—$2,400.

Winner, St. Louis Open, 269—$2,400.

Winner, Kansas City Open, won play-off from Doug. Ford and Dave Douglas—68–72–72—$2,400.